NAVAL WARSHIP
FSF-1
SEA FIGHTER

Steve White

Children's Press®
A Division of Scholastic Inc.
New York / Toronto / London / Auckland / Sydney
Mexico City / New Delhi / Hong Kong
Danbury, Connecticut

Book Design: Erica Clendening
Contributing Editor: Karl Bollers
Photo Credits: Cover, pgs. 6-7, ,26 © Mr. John F. Williams/U.S. Navy; pg. 4 ©
Sandy Huffaker/AP Photo; pg. 8 Getty Images; pg. 11 © James F. Gibson/AP
Photo/Library of Congress; pg. 12 Getty Images; pg. 14 © Heather Faulkner
/AFP/Getty Images; pg. 16 AP Photo/U.S. Navy; pg. 20 AFP/Getty Images; pg. 21
© Joe Raedle/Getty Images; pg. 22 AP Photo/U.S. Navy, Robert Catalano; pgs. 24-
25 © David Ree Morris/Reuters; pgs. 28, 39 Eli J. Medellin/U.S. Navy; pg. 30
Frederick McCahan/U.S. Navy; pg. 32 Douglas G., Morrison/U.S. Navy; pg. 34 ©
Jewel Samad/AFP/Getty Images; pg. 36 Philip A. McDaniel/U.S. Navy

Library of Congress Cataloging-in-Publication Data

White, Steve.
    Naval warship : FSF-1 Sea Fighter / Steve White.
    p. cm. — (High-tech military weapons)
    Includes bibliographical references and index.
    ISBN-10: 0-531-12091-0 (lib. bdg.)   0-531-18707-1 (pbk.)
    ISBN-13: 978-0-531-12091-0 (lib. bdg.)   978-0-531-18707-4 (pbk.)
    1. Sea Fighter (Ship)—Juvenile literature. 2. United States Navy—Weapons
systems—Juvenile literature. 3. Fast attack craft—United States—Juvenile
literature. I. Title. II. Series.

    VA65.Ş3975W485 2007
    623.825'8-dc22

                                                        2006015132

1 2 3 4 5 6 7 8 9 10 R 11 10 09 08 07

CONTENTS

The FSF-1 Sea Fighter was designed to operate effectively in waters very close to shorelines.

On a small island in Southeast Asia, terrorists have kidnapped tourists. After satellites locate their camp, a rescue mission gets underway. That night, a strange ship glides across the ocean toward the island.

An unmanned aerial vehicle (UAV) lifts off the ship's deck and zooms inland. An operator aboard the ship controls the UAV, ordering it to fly over the camp so he can view it through cameras that sense body heat. The ship approaches the island and slips into a shallow river mouth. A normal ship could not travel in water so shallow, but this isn't a normal ship. It is the Fast Sea Frame (FSF-1) Sea Fighter.

Two HH-60H Rescue Hawk helicopters, armed with machine guns, lift off from the Sea Fighter's deck. Soon, gunfire and explosions are heard as the helicopters swoop in and attack the terrorists' base. They rescue the tourists who are flown safely back to the Sea Fighter.

As the Sea Fighter moves away, its radar
picks up two terrorist speedboats approaching.
The terrorists attack. Aboard the Sea Fighter,
machine guns blaze, peppering the speedboats
with bullets. They soon sink beneath the waves.

The Sea Fighter launches cruise missiles at
the terrorist camp, now hundreds of miles away.
Satellites record events as the base is destroyed.

chapter 1

SEA FIGHTING: WHERE IT ALL BEGAN

On March 8, 1862, during the American Civil War (1861–1865), a strange-looking vessel approached the USS *Cumberland* and USS *Congress*, ships that belonged to the Union navy. This bizarre craft was the CSS *Virginia*, a warship of the Confederate navy, the enemy of the Union ships. The *Virginia* began firing at the *Cumberland* and the *Congress*, causing terrible damage. The return fire from the Union ships did not damage the *Virginia* at all. Their cannonballs bounced off because the *Virginia* was made of metal! The *Cumberland* and the *Congress* were made of wood. They stood no chance against the Confederate warship and were completely destroyed.

After the battle between the USS *Monitor* (left) and the CSS *Virginia* (right) ironclad sea vessels, navies around the world converted from wooden fighting ships to ships made of iron.

The *Virginia* had actually started out as a Union ship called the *Merrimack*, which had been sunk by the Union navy to prevent capture by the Confederates. The Confederates, though, discovered that the ship wasn't completely destroyed. They raised the *Merrimack*, rebuilt the wooden ship, covered it in metal, and renamed it CSS *Virginia*. It became the world's first "ironclad," a metal warship, and was armed with several types of cannons.

A NEW KIND OF VESSEL

The *Virginia*'s success against the *Cumberland* and the *Congress* terrified the Union navy, which sent out its own new ironclad, the *Monitor*. The *Monitor* looked like no other ship of the period. It was flat and looked like a sled. In its middle was a turret, a structure shaped like a drum that could swivel, or turn on the spot. The turret was armed with two very large cannons. All other ships at the time had their cannons lined up along their sides and they could not move. To hit a target, the whole ship had to turn so the cannons would be pointing in the right direction.

The crew of the USS *Monitor* take a break from duty to relax on her deck in this historic Civil War photograph.

The *Monitor* and the *Virginia* battled each other the day after *Virginia*'s historic victory. They exchanged cannon fire and tried to ram each other. In the end, the battle was a draw. This was the first fight between two metal warships. It marked the end of wooden sailing vessels. Soon, all warships were built of iron and steel, with their guns housed in moving turrets.

During World War II, aircraft carriers became a prominent feature of the U.S. Navy.

The most important of these were the giant battleships. Control of the sea depended on who had the best ones. Before World War I (1914–1918), the world's most powerful navy belonged to Great Britain. When World War II started (1939–1945), German aircraft and submarines threatened Britain's battleships. Even with all their guns and armor, the battleships proved to be easy targets for German torpedoes and bombs. The most important naval development during World

SEA BATTLES THROUGH HISTORY

Naval battles date back to the time of ancient Greece. The earliest one took place in 1210 B.C. near Cyprus.

The battle of Salamis, which took place in 480 B.C., saw 371 Greek ships defeat 1,271 Persian ships in what is possibly history's largest naval battle. Most of these ancient conflicts were fought with fast ships that used battering rams to sink enemy vessels. The ancient Romans would try to steer their ships close enough to opposing vessels to board them for hand-to-hand combat. This tactic was often used when long-range weapons could not defeat an enemy.

The USS *Ronald Reagan* is capable of carrying approximately six thousand crew members.

War II was the aircraft carrier, floating airfields that could transport dozens of planes. Aircraft carriers made it possible for warplanes to attack ships, sink subs, and bomb enemy land targets, all from hundreds of miles away, out at sea.

THE AGE OF THE AIRCRAFT CARRIER

By the end of World War II, there were fewer battleships and more aircraft carriers and submarines. By the 1960s, the carriers were huge, but they were very expensive to build. The biggest carriers belonged to America, which had the most powerful navy in the world. The latest one, launched in 2001, is the USS Ronald Reagan. It weighs over 100,000 tons (90,718 metric tons) and can carry about eighty-five aircraft. It cost five billion dollars to build.

Starting in the 1970s and 1980s, the U.S. Navy saw a gradual shift away from large, unwieldy ships. Aircraft carriers were simply too expensive and there weren't enough of them to go around. By the end of the twentieth century, the navy realized it needed a smaller, cheaper vessel that could swim upriver, close to shore, at night, in storms, and not be seen or heard while doing so.

The experimental X-Craft prototype was christened FSF-1 Sea Fighter on February 5, 2005.

X-CRAFT: BIRTH OF A SEA FIGHTER

T he idea for the FSF-1 Sea Fighter dates back to 1998, when the U.S. Navy asked the Titan Corporation to begin work on what was then called the X-Craft. The X-Craft was designed for a new style of naval warfare. In the 1960s and 1970s, the U.S. Navy was geared up to fight a possible war with Russia (then called the Soviet Union). Then the political climate in the Middle East shifted, and our attention shifted with it. Suddenly, the Middle East was a region that needed to be defended. Much of the oil vital to keeping America on the move comes from this part of the world. Huge oil tankers carried the oil from countries such as Saudi Arabia and Kuwait through a stretch of sea called the Persian Gulf.

Before the gulf spills out into the open waters of the Indian Ocean, it has to pass

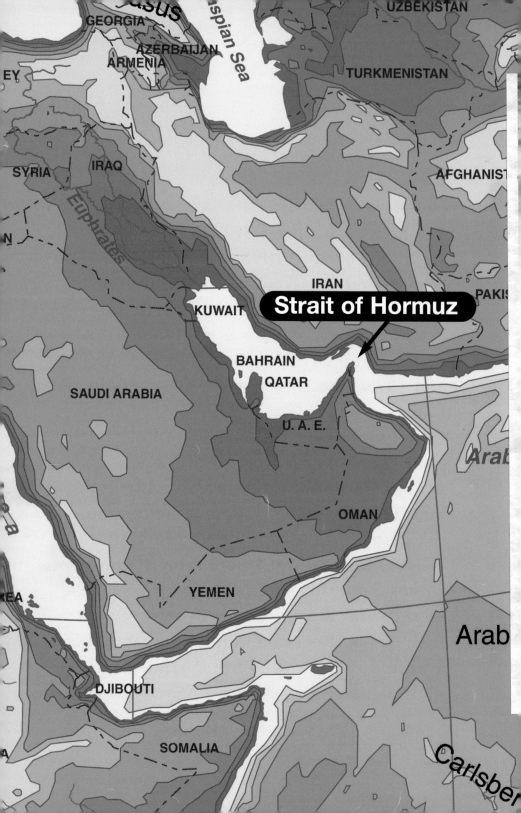

through a very narrow area called the Strait of Hormuz. Iran borders the strait. In 1979, a new government took power in Iran. Many countries in the Middle East were friendly to America, but the new Iranian government was not. Soon after taking power, it began threatening to close the Strait of Hormuz to oil tankers used by America and its allies.

The situation worsened when Iran became involved in a long and bloody war with its neighbor Iraq. This conflict spread to the gulf and oil tankers came under attack from both Iran and Iraq. The U.S. Navy began escorting the tankers, trying to keep the ships safe. The Iranian boats, though, were not typical warships. They were small speedboats carrying machine guns or cannons. The Strait of Hormuz was so narrow that these speedboats could dart out from the Iranian coast, attack oil tankers, and retreat before the navy warships could get anywhere near them. The best way to stop the speedboats was by using helicopters armed with weapons.

Much of the oil that is imported from the Middle East must travel through the Strait of Hormuz.

Here, Iranian army helicopters and navy boats take part in military practice drills in the Strait of Hormuz.

The Iranians also used mines, bombs placed underground or underwater. Because the strait was so narrow, the huge oil tankers could not avoid the mines. The U.S. Navy had a full-time job on its hands trying to keep the waters clear of these explosives. The U.S. Navy realized that it might need a new type of warship to help fight this kind of enemy.

By the late 1980s, Iran was letting tankers travel through the strait untroubled, but Iraq continued causing problems. These problems

made of aluminum, is 262 feet (80 meters) long, 66 feet (22 m) wide, and weighs around 950 tons (862 metric tons). It can also travel in just 11 feet (3 m) of water, far less than almost any other kind of warship. This makes it perfect for use in littoral, or coastal, waters.

25

Two years of research went into designing the hull of the FSF-1 Sea Fighter.

chapter 3

NAUTICAL BY NATURE: FIGHTER FEATURES

The top side of the Sea Fighter is mostly made up of a flat flight deck that can fit two helicopters, usually H-60 Seahawks. The Sea Fighter carries no weapons of its own. It has a large empty space inside called the mission bay. This area has been fitted to carry 20-foot (6 m) wide, boxlike containers called mission modules.

The Sea Fighter can carry up to twelve of these at any one time, and each has its own control panel. This means that different modules can be used for different missions. They are arranged and rearranged inside the Sea Fighter depending on the type of mission. These missions can include:

- anti-submarine warfare
- mine clearance
- landing soldiers on the shore and protecting them

- protection of other ships
- long-range cruise missile launches
- disaster support

To get equipment and cargo in and out of the mission bay, the Sea Fighter uses a ramp that swings up and down into the water. The ramp is in the stern, or back, and is fitted so that it can move small boats and underwater

Because the FSF-1 Sea Fighter is so fast and agile, it has often been compared to a sports car.

FLIGHT CLUB

The Sea Fighter is still in the experimental stage. If it ever becomes part of the U.S. Navy, it will be able to carry two helicopters. They will most likely be members of the H-60 Seahawk family. It is the navy's main helicopter, used for combat and rescue missions.

The SH-60 version of the Seahawk lifts off from a small warship, such as a destroyer. It has a three-man crew: a pilot, an airborne tactical officer (ATO), and a sensor operator, or "senso." The ATO organizes attacks on submarines and rescue missions. The senso uses the Seahawk's special equipment to locate submarines and ships.

The SH-60 has been very successful. Several versions of it are now in use, including:

- The HH-60H Rescue Hawk: a special combat search-and-rescue version that carries machine guns.
- The SH-60F Ocean Hawk: this helicopter is armed with torpedoes.
- The MH-60R: this newest type of Seahawk will hunt submarines and rescue people.
- The MH-60S Knighthawk: this truck-like version of the Seahawk family moves soldiers and supplies from one ship to another.

The Sea Fighter will be able to carry different versions of the H-60 depending on the mission.

The Sea Fighter is the first U.S. naval vessel to have a design based on a catamaran.

vehicles up to 36 feet (11 m) long in and out of the water, even while the boat is on the move.

The Sea Fighter is covered in a man-made, rubbery material called QuietShip that makes it very stealthy, or quiet. This substance actually reduces the amount of noise the ship makes by 70 percent!

The Sea Fighter uses two different types of engine to power it, a system known as Combined Diesel or Gas (CODOG). Two General Electric LM2500 gas turbine engines are used when the ship needs to travel at high speeds. Two MTU 16V 595 TE 90 propulsion diesel engines are used for low speeds. The CODOG engines also

power four Rolls-Royce Kamewa 125SII
waterjets. They help the Sea Fighter move
sideways, making it very agile. It can make
turns faster than most warships its size.

The CODOG engines are very powerful.
Even when fully loaded with equipment, the
Sea Fighter can go at 50 knots (58 mph, 93 kph).
In rough seas, with waves up to 7 feet (2 m) high,
it can still travel at 40 knots (46 mph, 74 kph).
With a full fuel load, the Sea Fighter has a
range of 4,000 miles (6,437 km). It can travel to
almost any trouble spot in the world without
the help of other ships. Most warships would
need to be refueled by tankers during such
lengthy trips.

The Sea Fighter's bridge was designed to accommodate a much smaller crew.

The Sea Fighter will have a crew of twenty-six that includes sixteen from the navy plus ten from the coast guard. Because the Sea Fighter has plenty of space for separate rest areas, its crew will include both men and women. A crew of twenty-six is unusually low for a standard warship. Even the most modern destroyers have crews of over one hundred, while aircraft carriers have crews of over one thousand!

The Sea Fighter crew is structured specially. Each crew member has more than one task. That means they have to understand all aspects of the ship, not just its engines, weapons, or electronics. The Sea Fighter's systems also help its crew. They are designed with automatic controls, ones that perform independently of operators. There are also many complex computers that monitor the

USS Abraham Lincoln on a relief mission in Indonesia.

ship's machinery and electronics. On older ships, humans would have performed these jobs.

The Sea Fighter will also use paperless navigation. Usually, ships use large paper maps to determine their location. Because the sea is such a huge area, many maps are needed as well as space to store them. Aboard the Sea Fighter, the Sperry Marine Electronic Charting and Display Information System (ECDIS) and the Voyage Management System (VMS) have replaced maps with simple-to-use computer screens.

FUTURE FIGHTING

At the moment, the FSF-1 Sea Fighter is a prototype, or an early model. Tests have proven the effectiveness of littoral-zone combat ships. They'll take warship capabilities into coastal waters for the first time. There they'll fight against enemies without navies or the usual types of warships.

The Sea Fighter will help the U.S. Navy prepare for the future. It will provide an idea of how tomorrow's naval vessels will look, making them more effective at fighting drug smuggling and helping ships in distress.

The U.S. Army is also interested in how well the Sea Fighter performs. It could be a far better way of getting soldiers into war zones.

Although the Sea Fighter currently has no weapons fitted, there are plans to arm it with an

The Sea Fighter may someday be loaded with surface-to-air medium-range missiles such as the Sea Sparrow.

affordable weapons system. Such a system might include a cheap cruise missile that will give it more firepower than an old battleship. Even with its tiny crew, it should be able to hit faraway targets with greater accuracy.

DANGEROUS WHEN ARMED

Currently, the FSF-1 Sea Fighter is unarmed. It can easily be fitted with weapons, though, so this may change in the future. Some of the weapons include:

• The AGM-84 Harpoon: this anti-ship missile has been fitted with its own radar, but can also use satellite guidance. The AGM-84 Harpoon is 15 feet (5 m) long and has a range of more than 60 miles (97 km). The Standoff Land Attack Missile (SLAM) version is used to attack coastal targets. It has a range of more than 150 miles (241 km).

• The SM-4 RGM-165 Land Attack Standard Missile (LASM): this version of the U.S. Navy's standard surface-to-air missile (SAM) has been fitted with satellite guidance and a warhead for attacking targets on land. It has a range of up to 200 miles (322 km).

• The Mark-45 5-inch gun: this is the U.S. Navy's standard gun for attacking targets ashore and for close-range fire against enemy vessels. It can fire 16 to 20 rounds per minute at a range of 13 miles (21 km).

A NAVY OF SEA FIGHTERS?

There is another problem facing standard warships–they aren't useful enough in current battles. Aircraft carriers still do the vital work of transporting bombers close to battle sites, but other ships like destroyers, guided missile cruisers, and submarines are left with nothing to do.

To be more effective against terrorism or rogue states such as North Korea, many people believe the United States needs a "brown water" navy that can operate much closer to shore. This navy could consist of Sea Fighters. For the cost of one eight-billion-dollar aircraft carrier, the navy could have fifty Sea Fighter warships.

The FSF-1 Sea Fighter promises to change the face of how battles are fought at sea.

FSF-1 SEA FIGHTER
At a Glance

Machine gun

Tactical Unmanned Aerial Vehicle

Hull

GENERAL CHARACTERISTICS

PRIMARY FUNCTION: LITTORAL WARSHIP	WIDTH: 66 FEET (22 M)
MANUFACTURER: TITAN CORPORATION	HEIGHT: 16' 8" (4.8 M, 20.3 CM)
COST: $79 MILLION	WEIGHT: 950 TONS (862 METRIC TONS)
SPEED: 50 KNOTS (58 MPH, 93 KPH)	CREW: TWENTY-SIX
WEAPONS: NONE; FUTURE—AFFORDABLE WEAPON SYSTEM CRUISE MISSILE AND MACHINE GUNS	POWER: TWO GE LM2500 GAS TURBINE ENGINES, TWO MTU 16-VALVE 595 TE 90 PROPULSION DIESEL ENGINES, AND FOUR ROLLS-ROYCE KAMEWA 125SII WATERJETS

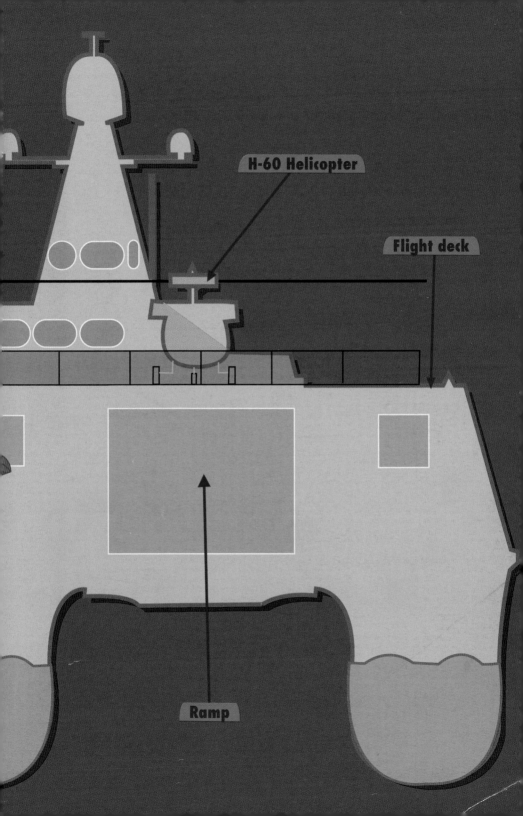

H-60 Helicopter

Flight deck

Ramp

automatic (aw-tuh-**mat**-ik) something that functions without anyone operating it

bow (**bou**) the front of a ship

"brown water" navy (**broun waw**-tur **nay**-vee) a fleet of warships that can operate close to shore

catamaran (kat-uh-muh-**ran**) a boat that has two hulls joined together with a platform on top

cruise missile (**krooz miss**-uhl) a missile that uses a guidance system to find its way to a target hundreds of miles away

destroyer (di-**stroi**-ur) a small, very fast warship that uses guns, missiles, and torpedoes to protect other ships from submarines

diesel (**dee**-zuhl) fuel used in diesel engines that is heavier than gasoline

firepower (**fire**-pow-uhr) capacity, as of a weapon, to deliver fire

NEW WORDS

flight deck (**flite dek**) the uppermost complete deck of an aircraft carrier

littoral (**li**-tuh-ruhl) near shore

mine (**mine**) a bomb placed underground or underwater

module (**mah**-jool) a separate, independent section that can be linked to other parts

prototype (**proh**-tuh-tipe) the first working model of a new machine

radar (**ray**-dar) a device that sends out radio waves that bounce off objects back to the sender and onto a display screen; used to see objects that are far away

stealth (**stelth**) secret and quiet

stern (**stern**) the back end of a ship

technology (tek-**nol**-uh-jee) the use of science or engineering to do practical things

FOR FURTHER READING

Crawford, Steve. *Twenty-First Century Warships: Surface Combatants of Today's Navies.* Osceola, WI: Motorbooks International, 2002.

Marriott, Leo, ed. *The Vital Guide to Modern Warships.* London: Airlife Publishing, Ltd., 2001.

Miller, David, ed. *The Illustrated Directory of Modern American Weapons.* Osceola, WI: Motorbooks International, 2002.

RESOURCES

ORGANIZATIONS

The National Civil War Museum
P.O. Box 1861
Harrisburg, PA 17105-1861
(717) 260-1861
www.nationalcivilwarmuseum.org

The United States Air Force
Chief of Public Relations
1040 Air Force Pentagon
Washington, D.C. 20330-1040
www.af.mil

The United States Navy
Chief of Information
Department of the Navy
1200 Navy Pentagon, Room 4B463
Washington, D.C. 20350-1200
www.navy.mil

RESOURCES

WEB SITES

HOW STUFF WORKS

http://science.howstuffworks.com/sea-fighter.htm
This fun site is packed with information on the FSF-1 Sea Fighter, complete with a lot of cool, colorful photos.

NAVAL HISTORICAL CENTER

www.history.navy.mil/
A detailed Web site on the history of the U.S. Navy dating back to the American Civil War.

THE U.S. NAVY

www.navy.mil/
The official Web site of the U.S. Navy.

INDEX

ABOUT THE AUTHOR

Steve White currently edits *Wallace & Gromit* and *Best of The Simpsons* for Titan Comics. In his spare time, he continues to develop his obsession with sharks, dinosaurs, and *The Simpsons*.